In a town far away
across the sea
something strange
occurred to me.

In this place
there were lots of cats
and every one of them
slept in a hat.

I thought to myself, "Why is this so?"
I racked my brains, I needed to know.

So I stopped a passing moggy to ask it:
"Why sleep in a hat, and not in a basket?"

"It all started with Fred," mewed the cat.

"The man on the hill who had hundreds of hats."

Fred had a hat for every occasion.
Large, tall, small,
some marvellous creations.

FANCY HATS

WOOLLY HATS

BANDANAS

SCARVES   GLOVES

Each afternoon
you'd see him in town...

In a fez at the deli,
at the bus stop, a crown.

Fred had a top hat,
a flat cap, a bonnet.

He had one from Australia
with corks hanging from it.

He wore hats with corners,
he wore them with pride.

He wore hats big and shiny
with bells on the side.

Fred loved to wear his red and blue Stetson when he was feeling country and western

His turban was gold,
his trilby was blue.
His bowler was spangly,
his beret was new.

His favourite hat was a glittery fedora,
he liked its wide brim and its magical aura.

One day at breakfast
Fred read in the news
that the town was holding
one of those royal dos

The Queen was coming.
Fred, excited at that,
decided to order
an extravagant
hat.

The biggest hat
that had ever been made,
covered in feathers,
sequins and braid.

Giant Hat Co.

"The finest hats for the finest of occasions"

~ NOW IN ~ The biggest hat ever made!

AS SEEN ON TV

Extravagant hats a speciality

FOR

Hat repair to order

Rise + shine Bakery to let, call

Maths tutor "Adds up to great value"

When the parcel arrived,
Fred was appalled.
The gigantic hat didn't fit at all!

There was no time to change it, what could he do?
He rushed down the hill, her Highness was due.

As fred stood in line
with hat over face,
he greeted her Maj
with a muffled "Your Grace."

The Queen was offended, couldn't hear what he said and so she ordered: "Off with his head."

I'm glad I stopped
the cat to enquire

but at the end of the tale

he started to tire

He explained that
he'd never been much of a talker

and curled up for the night

in his cosy deerstalker.

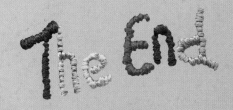

'Get Ahead Fred' is an original concept by Daisy Dawes

Author - © **Daisy Dawes**
Model Making - © **Daisy Dawes and Susan Dawes**

Photography - Steve Bicknell

The author would like to thank the following people for their support and inspiration: Rachel Fairfax, Susan, Holly, Eddie and Lesley Dawes, Foxy, Claudette Pearson, Steve Bicknell and everyone at Maverick.

PUBLISHED BY MAVERICK ARTS PUBLISHING LTD

©Maverick Arts Publishing Limited (2010)

Studio 4,
Hardham Mill Park,
Pulborough,
RH20 1LA
+44(0) 1798 875980

ISBN 978-1-84886-040-7

www.maverickartsclub.com